The Stoop and The Steeple

ISBN: 979-8-9880696-4-5 [First Paperback Edition]
ISBN: 979-8-3304-1261-7 [Second Paperback Edition]
ISBN: 979-8-9880696-5-2 [ePUB]

Library of Congress Control Number: 2024944513
I. Poetry   II. United States History   III. Memoir

Set in ITC Slimbach designed by Robert Slimbach for Monotype
with heads in Eliza Text designed by David Sabino from Blackletra
text citations in Broadsheet from Three Islands Press
and Elizabeth's diary excerpts set in Lamar Pen from Three Islands Press.

Cover design by Isa Fernandes in collaboration with Camilla Monk
and Stephanie Pressman.
Back cover photo by Joss Ettrick.

All proceeds from the sale of this book will support research and education
at the Porter-Phelps-Huntington Foundation. https://www.pphmuseum.org

THE STOOP AND THE STEEPLE

NANCY L. MEYER

Frog on the Moon
A small press
Cupertino, California
September 27, 2024

DEDICATED TO

Elizabeth Porter Phelps my 8th-Great-Grandmother
whose diary helped me see myself

Elizabeth's Diary and Glasses, Porter-Phelps-Huntington Museum, Hadley MA

1753 when the cock was placed at the top of the steeple Zeb Prutt ascended to the summit, sat on the copper bird and imitated the crowing of a rooster.

—Sylvester Judd, *History of Hadley*, 1863

I can't stop seeing Zebulon on the steeple, hearing his call singe the sky. I can't stop knowing my own ancestors enslaved him.

Zeb cockadoodling over the churchgoers, bonnets and flat-tops askew, scuttling out of their fresh-hewn pews, the pine still pungent. Hands shading eyes, *Look. It's Widow Porter's African man.*

I picture him shining like the copper rooster, his sweat-bright skin dark against a white steeple. Do his thighs burn, clinging up there? Does the rooster screech, chafing on its iron rod? I want Zebulon heroic, crowing for freedom.

From bare shoulders, I want him to spring iridescent feathers, green, red, black. I want him to wing out his arms, swoop onto the breast of clouds. Soar beyond the honking vee of geese, down the Great River flashing blue. Away from my enslaving 8th great grandmother. Fly, fly away Zebulon.

Irony. He still serves me, shining and crowing in my head. Pries my voice from white pages. Demands I look at every pore and scar of my own skin, what I do to him, what we do to each other.

At my feet, a Rhode Island Red scratches in the dirt with yellow claws. Stirs the soil.

Introduction

Journal Note 2018

I'm 75 years old when I learn for the first time that my Pilgrim ancestors "owned slaves." One of them even captained a slave ship from Grenada as late as 1808 when such trade was illegal. He drowned en route and part of me is glad though I grieve for all who were lost.

Written in family diaries, inventories, even one letter from an enslaved man, himself. I never read them. No one talked. Even though I often drove by the big white farmhouse, now a museum. Even though the names Porter, Phelps, Huntington rang through my childhood. Even though Gramma took us for picnics on the long back porch where the enslaved and servants ate. Farmers, artists, teachers: those are the only stories I knew.

It was my mother's mother whose ancestors arrived in 1639. Their heyday in the 1700's as founders of the town of Hadley, Massachusetts. But the Gramma I knew owned three housedresses and one good frock, stretched a roast for most of a week, boiled her own soap. She fought for Sacco and Vanzetti in her 30's, against McCarthy in her 60's, ran a nursery school into her 80's.

Owning people, selling people, tearing families apart, getting status and property and wealth to pass along because of the slave labor of men, women and children who lived under our roofs, people whose names are listed in inventories with the cattle and snippets of stories in a 16-year-old daughter's diary about a boy she grew up with but refers to as a "man owned by my father."

I have been retelling this story so I can make it real. So I can see who I am without excuses. So I can be seen, without hiding. But the story is not about me. It is about how we created the society at the origins of the United States, how we keep it that way, and how we must change it.

Journal Note 2024

This energy launched my project but is not where the poems led me. Only when I decided to focus on Zebulon, one man we enslaved. Only when I learned he was light skinned. Like Mel, my first husband, a Jamaican man with African, Scots and Dutch ancestors. Only when I touched the shards of that relationship, felt the pain of the permanent separation that now exists between him and the family we created together. Only then could I complete this book.

That I was slow to realize this connection is a sign of white bias. I saw only our personal issues and lost focus on the impact of race and power in our marriage. I continue to notice the intergenerational impact on all of us: black, mixed and white. Looking deeply, as I have these past seven years, brought me healing and hope. I publish this writing to inspire others to find their own portals so together we can build a more inclusive world.

Contents

I. The Stoop

The Stoop: 1964

All day I sit on the brown stone,
stained sticky with sno-cone
drips; or is this junkie's blood?

He isn't home. First day
with his new puppy, maybe
he forgot our date.

I'm not leaving.

Ukrainian lady, wide-hipped
in apron and babushka, limps down,
shuffles off to buy cigarettes.

Puerto Rican family bumps a tilting
grocery cart up each step. Overripe
plantains perfume the six dim flights.

I'm not leaving.

At last I spot him loping down
the block, baby black and brown Dober
bounces ahead. Mel's hair short, tee shirt tight.

Even better in daylight, his glide, his eyes—glossy
chestnuts. Jump up in my blonde pony-tail
and gypsy blouse. Did you forget? I blurt.

Off guard, he smiles, holds
the door for me. We climb five
floors, bathtub in the kitchen.

I'm still not leaving.

He quotes Gibran, studies art
with Salvador Dali, grew up
in Canada, with ice skates,

tennis and skis like me. Born
Jamaican, not African-American.
Besides, he gets a hard-on

the minute I unbutton my jeans.

Alone

I hear in jail they beat you
with soap in a sock so the bruises
don't show. I ride South alone
on the Greyhound.

After Bloody Sunday, Bull Connor,
dog's yellow teeth. The New York
charter buses, fiancé Mel's carpool
all left. Now I sit prim

in my navy-blue sheath
as though it will protect me.
Lurch through the night, over
the Mason-Dixon line. Five AM,

rest stop, Macon, Georgia.
Locals leer as I pick at
watery grits, white and slick.
On to Selma, up the rise

of the Pettus Bridge. Tanks
skulk below, slits for windows,
faceless. Soldiers, bayonets. Is this
America? Step off the bus.

Hushed houses. Trees lush, lawns trim. Where's
Brown Chapel? I plead under my breath
to a lone black gardener who nods
the direction, stiff as a bird.

Sidewalk slides to clay. Ahead
sign-up tables, food lines. I swirl
into the welcome rumple, a black
and white flock. Join the March, 6 abreast

53 miles, 5 days to Montgomery.
Ain't Gonna Let Nobody Turn Us Round.
I sing from my feet, from all our feet.
Talk and sing, arm in arm.

We believe, even though
the National Guard, who pockmark
the fields, point their guns at us. We
believe even though we sweep for

landmines before camping in the open,
tarps over muddy ground. Glimpse Dr. King,
circles under his eyes. Nursing blisters,
we talk and sing into the night.

Day Two, passing a shack, I hear
the man who lived there was killed
in front of his kids, registering
voters here in Lowndes County.

Matrons limp on, Sunday dresses,
curled-over pumps. School boys wear
starched shirts; only we whites
can afford to be casual.

By the time we press into Montgomery,
half the speeches are over. Every black person
out on their porches cheers us on;
we tromp through their unpaved

mud to Courthouse Square. Martin's
voice dim on loudspeakers.
Thousands have flown, driven, walked in.
TV cameras, shoulder to shoulder, we sway

We Shall Overcome—but are warned run,
run for the black part of town the minute
the rally's done. No cops will protect;
the Guard disbanded. Cars of thugs rev

against dispersing crowds, gun barrels braced
on rolled-down windows. That night word spreads,
the Klan killed Viola Liuzzo driving alone
over our chant-filled road.

6 AM, solo again on the Greyhound, my silent hum:
Keep Your Eyes On The Prize. They still pull folks
like me off buses into the swamps hung
with Spanish moss.

There are none of the human race too low & despicable for God to bestow Salvation upon. Yea it is the mean & base things of this world which God is pleas'd to elect to eternal life...

Servants who are at the dispose & Command of others Who, it may be are despised in the world, may be the Lord's freemen and heirs of glory.

What a temptation for the Devil is it therefore to lead Servants in to Sin and provoke God; to insinuate into them they ought not to bide in ye place of Servant.

I ask myself, what stories do I tell today that keep all of us in our place?

Loose leaf, first page missing

Where we didn't marry in Mississippi to test the anti-miscegenation laws. Flank to flank in Mel's sleeping bag, a soggy Selma field. Whisper, *should we?* Even the euphoria of the March, even the leaders asking us, we don't dare.

Staring Match

Mel's Aunt Lilla insists we meet in a coffee shop far from her doorstep. Mel, his mom Joyce, and I can't stop staring at her long bleached hair, pressed straight, above layers of pancake makeup, slender nose. She glares at Mel's Afro, her sister Joyce's curl twisting free on a brown neck. *You're so pretty,* Lilla eyes my sleek blond page boy. She passes for white on Long Island. Joyce refuses to invite her to the wedding.

Painting the Doll

Muggy August day in suburban Weston MA. *Head back, hold still.* Bill at the picnic table with his bottles and brushes. I never wear make-up. He curls my lashes. Soft finger-rubs of blush sculpt my cheeks. My lids he feathers grey-blue to match my eyes. I keep blinking, wooden as my childhood doll, Aurora Borealis.

The Only Women in Gowns

Joyce sewed her own. Vaunts honey-brown arms in sleeveless, full-length, lavender silk. Matching wide brimmed straw. Her daughter in yellow turban and spike heels—toucans bright against the oaky green. I failed to alert them to our more casual dress code, don't track the covert glances, count the *oohs* over Joyce's Jamaican lilt.

Dad Poses with His Women

My wedding dress—short linen, bodice pink and beaded—I buy at a Madison Avenue shop with my Jewish grandmother. All the customers over 60. She pulls a pastel Chanel from her closet to button over her corset. My mother wears fuchsia shantung from Filene's that drains the color from her face. Beaming for the camera, Dad yokes his arms around our shoulders. Mom already knows he's cheating.

The Wedding Party

Navy suit drapes Mel's supple frame. Our friends show up in tie-dye, silver belt buckles, scarves and bolos. Gay. Straight. Coupled. Not. One lives out of his car, another in a cabin upstate. Only now, turning these pages it hits me—all of them, white.

Grey Stone and Ivy

Easier if it rains, Mom said. Here we are huddled in the Unitarian Church, under its arched shadows, Bach tremolos—most of us atheists. My Yankee grandmother's white hair strays from a loose bun under her one felt hat, brushed clean of cat fur. Jewish side of the family in knits and pearls check out the hymnals. The only ones to say aloud, *What if your children turn out to be black?*

White Joint

Hideous Highway 128 Holiday Inn. Filet mignon instead of a picnic. *It's our party,* we tried to censor my parents' guest list. Dad insists, *Invite them or people will think we're hiding.* They clump tight, voices low, acrid wisps of Chanel #5. We tune them out, sneak a hit out back, white Zig Zag paper, the white joint we pass.

Two Hands

Joyce bakes us a Jamaican wedding cake laced with dark rum. Not the three-tiered one we cut, two hands on the knife, white plastic bride and groom teetering.

Dark fruit cake bedded under thick butter cream. So much rum it lasts for years. Tradition is to eat a slice at your wedding. We ate alone in the car driving north to our cliffside honeymoon in Cape Breton. Three years later, another slice in a Brooklyn kitchen for the birth of our brown-gold son Adam, not quite the Christening ritual. Mel's mom Joyce must have kept the remains: in her blue gown at Adam's wedding 25 years later, she pulls him aside, places in his hands a soft square cocooned in linen, stained brown with 200 proof Appleton. I see him cringe before thanking her then slide it in the trash without showing his bride. I wonder, will he ever accept this gift?

October 11, 1772. brought my offer — a first born son. Tis the Lords.

Even with the baby live in your arms you call him "it:" How scared were you?

I worried 'til I counted 10 toes, 10 fingers but I didn't expect either of us to die.

On Apple Valley's long dirt road,
our geodesic dome blared electric-blue.
We bought a beat-up hearse for a camper,
then bedded it with straw for our goose
after the fox killed his mate. Thought we hid
the pot plants between our corn stalks;
their spiky green canopied two feet taller.
Homemade root beer exploded in the pantry;
pink and blue fungus tentacled out of the root cellar.
I went to India for 6 weeks, leaving Mel
to wrestle our 4-year-old into his snowsuit
down the hill to the school bus, yellow beacon
in waist high snow. Long-haired friend, back
from Nepal, lived with us that winter, barefoot.
We built a teepee for a peyote meeting,
fed the fire, drummed and sang through the night—
first time I believed in god. Under a full moon
we rode the motorcycle, headlights off.
Startled the heifers by lying in their meadow
to look at the stars. They circled close,
black nostrils snuffing and blowing. Our heads
buzzed in the clover, lofting us above
fresh cowpies or church supper gossip.

Cheese, cheese, hay, hay, cooking, cooking, churning every other day sometimes—I have had two days now, that I have indulged myself in bed till near 5, but tomorrow morning it must be a little after 3 that the butter may be worked in the cool air... I do not have time for thots and reflection...[iii]

Elizabeth, I like your ditty. Tugging against duty.

1968
Mel, when the garage guy calls you *Boy,*
my white mouth quips at you, *Don't get angry.*
I grab these words like a switch.
You bite your lip.

1970
Geodesic dome, harpsichord parties
under apple trees. I put up 3 dozen
jars of tomatoes; you put Pink Elephant
blotter acid on your tongue.

1972
This snow, this hemlock, these hills
my home not yours. We talk
it over. I say, *Go find your desert, your*
wild land, your known.

1973
Months, you roam Ethiopia, Somalia.
Come home, *Let's eat with our hands.*
Pinch stew in a hunk of bread
tuck it between our lips.

1974
Move to Kingston. Our 4-year-old fails
to mouth, *Yes Miss,* to his Jamaican teacher.
Miss Vidal-Smith canes his bare
brown legs. Welts rise.

1977
Move to San Francisco: proud dad, you
demo dashiki and drums for son's class.
After that, kids jeer *Jigaboo, jungle monkey!*
at our blonde-haired boy.

1980
I moved out this morning, you say.
Like that, after 15 years.
I, speechless on the kitchen stool,
both of us bawling.

four feet below   black daggered sea urchins   hundreds   pock
    white sand   mask faulty   burbles full   i gasp   no
                     air   no place to stand

thrash the turquoise sea   we moved here on purpose
    raise our son in his father's land
                Circle the surface, Mel instructs

then free-dives forty feet   eye-sure   through
    coral lattice   rose and sapphire   spear-gun cocked
    silver tails flick   he bursts up   brandishing

a parrot fish   strings it on the wire loop i trail behind me
    each fish hangs   a bloody flag   i worry about sharks
    he dives again

i hold my position   white flesh   alien sea   test
    the salt   pray   it buoys me over   what teems   below
    i must find   a mask that fits

Higglers[*]

Early cool of day, the women
set down baskets brimmed with yam,
breadfruit, tomato and callaloo.
Spread their piece of cloth,
change purse lashed snug
in a skirt pocket. *Mawnin'*
to their sister higgler, if they're not
quarreling over something.

See me coming, white gal
from University housing, pony tail
to my waist. Truth is their head ties,
patois, cave-black faces scare me.
Only fair they make me pay
for all of Colonialism in the price of
one star-apple.

Rebeccah's mangoes are sweetest.
Gold specks surprise me, glinting from her sepia
eyes. Truffle-dark skin dusted white
at elbow and heel—too much sun,
not enough time to rub in
a little cocoa butter. I stop at her cloth
every day, tell her my name.

Finally muster, *Chaw, you k'yan ask*
that much for one scrawny cah-rot
my Jamaican accent hovers. Rebeccah
chuckles, throws in three more. *Walk*
good, she smiles.

---

* Higglers – Pronounced Igglers. Derived from the archaic verb "to higgle" meaning to haggle or to bargain, these are the vendors and marketers that form the backbone of Jamaica's internal market system.

A Bloody Jamaican Hero

Parboosingh paints with the fury of white rum, 200 proof Appleton.
His living room tiles, a confetti of one-inch rags black, red, white,
blue, who needs a carpet?
He loves our four-year-old son, whirlwind of blonde curls.

We find Parboo on his bathroom floor blood exploding the walls, red
against porcelain, black beard red.

Two rules at our son's school: No throwing green mango. No cussing bad-word.
Teacher overhears, "bloody man." Four whacks of the ruler on his little hand.
Color leaches out.
I fume into the principal's office, white on black.

Rum will burst your esophagus once the liver's gone.
A week in ICU, tearing at his tubes. White light, white every
corner, sheet and wall.
Even dead, the artist rages. Slathers, stabs
Windsor red, Cadmium red, magenta, mauve.

Artist residency and a one-man show. Welcome home
son of Jamaica. Mel moved away when he was 10.

We learn to drive on the left, don't bite Scotch Bonnets, ungarble the lilt of patois, tuck
in the mosquito net; how long to soak salt cod.

Step into dim-lit shacks with friend Martha, U.N. mental health counselor. Children
chained to beds, locked in sheds.

Uncles Eric and Colville invite us to Sunday dinners, shower us with
backyard breadfruit and mangos.

Dance with the Maroons high in the "cockpit" mountains. Come home
itching with grass lice.

We begin to notice only people with 'bright" skin and "good" hair
are the bank tellers, secretaries, on TV.

The color line tricks Mel, his blossoming Afro, blonde son, American accent. Doors
open
a crack, then close.

Young Bob Marley lives up the street. *I Shot the Sheriff*…Rasta rallies in the park.
Woodsy
smoke from spliffs fat as firecrackers.

Black Pride a match striking a damp box. Only 10 years since Independence,
the girdle of British rule. Half the people

worship Haile Selassie, half wave tiny flags for the Queen.
Mel is not alone. Everyone's identity a jumble of jackstraws.

Prime Minister Manley pays the poor to hand-sweep streets.
Mel gets mural commission for the Bank of Jamaica.

We decide to stay.

Bus bumps and jars me to deep rural villages; I teach family planning
to 12-year-olds. They teach me a baby, the only dream they see.

Transfer our son from cane-switching, rote-teaching Mona Prep
to Priory, expat kids of execs, field trips and poetry.

Red-haired Scots and an Indian-Jamaican boy, our son's best friends.
Mel shows them how to catch lizards with a noose

of thread. I find comfort with other mixed-race couples, the most
we've ever known.

Mel represents Jamaica at FESTAC arts festival in Nigeria;
returns delirious with malaria.

OPEC oil embargo. Gas $5 a gallon, store shelves empty. U.S.
drivers line up at the pump, rant about the jump from 38¢ to 55.

We make cooking oil from coconuts, drain bacon on newspaper,
only cold water for dishes. The barefoot man

begs on our corner. I get free tuition
for a Masters at the University of the West Indies.

Bars on our windows. If the skull can squeeze through,
any size body can wriggle in. One tries.

Our son sings in *Joseph and the Technicolor Dreamcoat*. Splits
his brow slipping at a pool. ER orderly pins him down; stitches

with a re-used needle. Mel gnaws curry-goat
on the beach with artists who can't afford canvas or paint.

Swills port on lawns with elite ones courting overseas buyers.
Art world politics contort, island-tight.

We find Parboo on the bathroom floor. Blood fountains
the walls, fingerpaints white tiles red. His profligate liver

burst; he dies, raging, in the ICU. Mel's work dries up.
I lose my job. Three weeks, sell all we can, land

in San Francisco. Local school, white kids bused in.
Our son's class is crowded, two years behind Priory.

We have no black friends.

I can't stop
seeing

Zebulon on
the steeple,
hearing his
call singe
the sky. I
can't stop
knowing
my own
ancestors
enslaved him.

Patoos Croon in the Frangipani Tree

Red ginger blossoms, flanks
of banana leaves rustle
against white burglar bars guarding
our bedroom windows—flung wide
to the Jamaican night.

Under the froth of mosquito net,
my love's dusky leg scrubs across
my pale one, pins me to damp sheets.
I ramble through his springy hair. Full
lips search my thin ones. Our teeth clack.

Sweat and slide in the tousled night. Slowly,
tongue the ribs of his mouth, his nipples,
traverse the firm terrain of belly
as it drops off into deep shoals.
I swim in the surge.

He perspires raindrops onto my breasts,
licks the salt from my skin and
coaxes open sea anemone petals
before we plunge into the oceans
that divide us.

Out of Many, One People
Jamaican national motto

Orange bougainvillea drapes our veranda.
    Petals flutter skin-thin over an ambush of thorns.
        Outside our bedroom, banana leaves conspire.

Your nose long and flared like my grandfather's. Mango juice
    goldens both our chins, runs down my white arm, your
        red* one. We don't look that far apart, yet

ghosts hang in the air the night we stay at the plantation,
    cling tight on mildewed sheets. Below, a dungeon, broken
        chains, rusted rings. Rain plinks on tin. A metronome.

Hard enough to scour empty grocery shelves, live without
    a telephone, friends dropping by for rum at all hours,
        find a job, again.

Ackee and saltfish in Uncle Colville's backyard, dark under
    a 50-foot breadfruit tree. His skin high-yellow,
        the shade of the green fruit's creamy innards.

You tilt a hip like a resting horse—consider the palette, thrust
    a sable brush into a wallop of acrylic. Fast strokes on
        canvas, black faces, red bus, windshield opaque.

History scrolled on all our skins, but you and I never murmured
    about our color over candlelight, didn't
        rhyme or dance those stories with our son.

* Caribbean word for brown skin, light enough to pass for white

Grieve But Cannot Grieve

after Rodney Jones, *How Much I Loved This Life*

You rise in the light, blistered by light.
Jamaica 1974, we live in the yeast
of Black is Beautiful.

Every moment we scrape awake.
If I lay my hand on your arm, you
jump as if a *duppie* swept over you.

We cringe in our bed
from the reggae band thumping
all night across our back fence

splintering ears that refuse to listen.
You rise in the light, blistered by light.
Is it the cleft of continents,

undertow of the slave trade
that sears you?
I rise in the light

blistered by your light
that pokes like a detective
into my shadows.

Our Love Blew Apart Like a Piñata

I crawled madly in the grass   grabbing   pieces

stuffing them in my mouth   sticky   into my pockets.   I licked
          the sweet ones

               over and over:

          our son curly and blonde,
the day we bolted the last 2x4 on the geodesic dome

          spear-fishing a meal   of parrot fish
          when we waved goodbye—you to Africa

                    me to India—

     swept into each other's arms
                         coming home full of stories.

The sour pieces   I left

               moldering on the ground until

          I could bear the taste.

Zeb

c
o
c
k
a
d
o
o
d
l
i
n
g
over
the
churchgoers,
bonnets and
flat-tops askew

The day you left me. The day after Reagan won. *To find myself,* you sobbed.
No word of the other woman.

Our pre-teen son wailing on his waterbed. Me staggering into work
the next day to teach Stress Management.

No arms like when you caught our boy flying off the careening wagon. No
forehead for me to bathe when you raged with dengue fever.

No black-white couple marching, no liberated roles. My posters tattered,
discarded after the demonstration.

She understands me, you said of your sculptor girlfriend.

*Yeah, but who works 12-hour days, a 3-hour commute, pays the mortgage
on our matchbox house, sells Amway at night to build our son's college fund?*

Almost 50 years now, I see that I had already left you,
the man you were, the life you visioned.

Last I heard you live solo in a sod house on a Taos mountain, winter
in your van on a Mexican beach. You have not spoken

to our son or grandchildren in eighteen years. Choose not to walk through
their Silicon Valley door with your shaved head and sandals.

Recant

Mel called himself mulatto,
so I did too. Thought
it simply named the fact: two
white grandparents, two black.

Not the word for "mule,"
for what comes
of a horse and donkey fucking.

I think he absorbed it below
the skin, whiplashed by
doors that opened
to his white-appearing face:
slammed against an indelible smear.

Summers as a porter
on the Canadian Railroad,
Sir, may I shine your shoes?
Earning college tuition.

Now I hear the slurs I missed:
Dirty   Sterile   Hybrid   Half-Caste

Swallow the barbed "mulatto." Say
mixed, mixed race. I don't know
If I'm fooling myself, that removing
this tiny splinter will ease any pain.

I do know my ribcage expands and
I feel safer that I will cause less harm.

him
shining
like the copper
rooster

Do his
thighs
burn,
clinging
up there?
Does the
rooster
screech,
chafing
on its
iron rod?

Two Marriages

1984-present: Chris

        you dazzle up in a bronze Porsche   went to Camp Androscoggin
                same as my Dad

your mind snaps logical like his   our two bodies
    clip in place snug as Legos   your mom lives

        blocks from my upper East Side grandmother   lure
    of the familiar   I leap to you   like a trout

engaged in 3 months we clamber the jungle gym
    of blended family   teenage boys and exes

        build our hilltop home   bevies of quail under
                fuchsia oleander before long   five   grandkids   scurry

        we whir the world on bicycles   pedal Tourmalet and Stelvio
           dive   under oceans from Kona to Kas   our scuba

                    bubbles lull   reliable
our rhythms   slow

                grooves mapped deep   family deaths
        cast a silvery sheen   the underside of leaves

              every moment tallied   I am not afraid
              to gaze through our years   a lava lamp

    love scarlet   violet   hurts   dissolve   turn to
            mossy green   eels of color

daffodils yellow   blue gentians sprawl our son naps
on the back steps   in the box the stereo came in
he does have a crib   painted turquoise

wood bars   strong   against his stand-up rocking
bellowing for   the pacifier   tossed to the floor   of course
he throws it   again   didn't we all cry

white geese   rhubarb leaves   geodesic dome   golden
parsnips dug from frost   I sing Hindu chants in   India
pray at the feet   of a giant Buddha

you sketch village barbers in Sudan
fall in a manhole in Mogadishu
crave yam and callaloo

star apples dangle pale   we fail   to root in your Jamaica.
Little League in bone-cold fog   banana slugs glide ochre
even in San Francisco we never fit

Fall

Once we lived among apple trees.
Tapered ladders tipped into two-toned leaves.

Red fruit, we twisted stem from branch,
set each side by side in gathering bags.

Never drop them or they'll bruise
the farmers warned us.

Our son, tee-shirted in a red wagon
flew too fast down the rutted hill

catapulted into air.
You leapt in time, rolled him in your arms.

Forty years on   you slipped each other's hold
Grown father   grown son   How did you spin apart?

Barren space between you

II. The Steeple

Ice, miles-thick, the world groaned under it. No life moved. A crack, an ooze. The ice began to melt and like a turtle from the mud, the earth rose, barren as the turtle's shell. Creamy-blue was Lake Algonquin that grew from glaciers' flow, so cold no fish could survive. Beavers big as black bears, Pocumtuck legend tells, dammed the lake, before it drained away creating the River Quenecticut. Lichen, spruce, deer found a toehold. Pequot ancestors followed, 11,000 years ago. To the place called Nonotuck "midst of the river," they walked, pitched their wigwams, in the meadow Capawonk, caught trout in the clear waters of Nepasoancage running down Mt. Quunkwattchu. They planted corn in Wequittayyngg. Honored their dead below Mt. Wequomp, the blocky prominence resembling a giant beaver. A man-eating, insatiable beaver who ate all the plants until the people complained to god Hobomok who clubbed it with a tree trunk so it died in the great lake and turned into their stone mountain. Hunt, fish, move on after reaping chestnuts, year upon year. Until their sachems Chickwollop, Umpanchella and Quonquont sold the land to John Pynchon and the strange white men, my ancestors, moving up the river.

1659

Back when the 49 founders followed
their Calvinist gospel. Back when
they laid out 8 acre lots with care that no one
had better land than another. Back
when my ancestor Samuel Porter
built the modest house on Middle Street
and everyone's cows grazed
in the Commons. Back then
they still honored the contracts with
the Pequot and Abenaki who sold them
the land. Welcomed them every spring
to plant corn, fish the Quinnecticut,
and a few stayed on, sold baskets and brooms.

1704

Back when the Sumptuary Laws forbade
gold rings and lace collars, lest God
punish them with war and pestilence. Back
when my forebears got rich trading furs
down the river. That's when others
pointed fingers, named them *River Gods.*
Back when, one snowy night, the French led
Mohawk and Pocumtuck to attack Deerfield,
right next door. When they killed 48 townsfolk,
captured 140 in under 2 hours.

1752

Back when Samuel's grandson Moses acquired
600 acres beyond the Commons. Back when
he built his grand house, with a four-flued chimney
and rusticated cladding. Back when the Abenaki
returned to plant corn and found fencing

and dogs to run them off. Back when, two years later,
Captain Moses Porter was killed in the ambush
of Bloody Morning Scout.[iv] And Porter's Pequot body
servant delivered his sword to my 9th-great-
grandmother Elizabeth, who took to laudanum
and rocking in a darkened room.

I inherit Mom's copy of *Forty Acres* when she dies at 98. Slim volume, even so, it jams my bookshelf. Gramma's cousin, Jimmy Huntington, wrote it. Moses Porter, my 9th-great-grandfather, built it, 1752. Said to be first house outside the stockade, that protected our Hadley, Mass. founders. *Forty Acres,* towering elms and single black shutters. 200 years we lived there, Cousin Jimmy the last. I played on the stoop, rolled in the grass.

Genealogies, antiquities, I never cared. Until these words, cataloged without comment:

> an inventory for the Estate of Cap't Moses Porter, March 8, 1756. Cash 3£ 5s, Negro man £400... Zebulon Prutt, the son of Arthur, a slave, belonging to the Reverend Isaac Chauncy, pastor of the Church in Hadley... This slave boy must have been the property of the parson's daughter for she sold him to Moses Porter ... 29th of July, 1745

Minister. Ancestor. Women. Buying and selling   people. And then, this:

> .... when the cock was placed at the top of the steeple, Zeb Prutt, a young colored man, ascended to the summit, sat on the copper bird and imitated the crowing of a rooster.

I know this church. The steeple, 90 feet high.

Gramma never told us these stories, no Zebulon on the steeple. Never, even when I married an African-Jamaican man. Mother never said our cow-milking, broom-corn-planting, Harvard-attending family were also slave-owning. Even when we raised a son only miles away. I must tell him, his children. I spin like the rooster. Us, enslavers. A man crowing. A man who hoed the sod where we just buried my mother.

I dream

a gun   fixed to my hand
black barrel   pointing out
metal hot   cries bottled   in its throat

In the dream

my palm open like a platter   pistol presses its steely weight
my wrist   bends back   my fingers   will not close

In the dream I squall

how did this gun get here   i don't   believe   in guns
father responds   we've always
had it   under the car seat

Still-dreaming mind scrambles

i've driven this car for years   my heels so close
to the gap   never   reached under   never groped
the dark   felt the handle

In the dream I yell at my family
take this gun   i don't want it   take it

Violently awake
i shake my wrists, my hands
my fingers

Porter-Phelps-Huntington House

I

Two hundred-seventy-two years ago,
the most elegant in Hadley.

Green front door framed by wavy glass.
Now white clapboards graying,

May-October a straggle
of museum-goers ogle

my ancestors' portraits,
too many Elizabeths.

They don't see interns whir
winter dust with a vintage Electrolux,

don't see the annual unwrapping of
patched quilts, threadbare sheets

pulled from mahogany
tables, sideboards, cradles.

Pewter polished, silver laid
as if someone still lived there.

II

The house a map. A fingerprint
still visible on the lead tea caddy

Major-General Lincoln used
in the Revolutionary War.

Floorboards milled from local
200-year-old pine, the smell of

smoked pork clings to the clay oven,
hundreds of footsteps indent

the central hall stairs. Mary Huntington
used her diamond ring to etch her name

in the front bedroom window,
last visit before typhus took her.

III

Gramma dragged me here, age 8.
Cobwebby smell, iron kettle big

as a church bell swung in the fireplace.
Rough tables on the back veranda, we

picnicked on peanut butter sandwiches
with grainy honey. Gramma never

said the laborers—enslaved,
indentured, apprenticed —

slurped pease porridge and greens
sitting on these very benches.

IV

Captain Moses Porter's sword,
I touched it.

Same one his Pequot servant
passed through the window

to Elizabeth, putting her daughter
to bed. Oh, the moans that night

Her Captain dead, 1754. Ambush
of Bloody Morning Scout.

V

Docents tell of the enslaved
child of the enslaved daughter of

the enslaved Peg Bowen. Carried
by another Elizabeth from the dank

straw of her cellar bed. Covered in
sores, fevered. Laid deep

in a six-slab chest by the fire
so she'd be warm, safe from embers.

Dead that night. From King's Evil.
I stroke the rust-hued wood

lid closed.

*February 1782, "Thursday my husband
and I up to Mr. Arams' at Muddy
Brook. He a seventh son—we took Phillis
with us—think she has a Kings evil."*[iv]

Elizabeth, biographers
name your kindness
to baby Phillis
despite enslaving her;

              kind to bring her up
              from the freezing cellar;
              build a chest to keep her warm;

kind to drive the carriage up to Mr. Aram
for laying on of hands;

     after her funeral, held in your Long Room
     you write: *a very pretty Child,
I hope she sleeps in Jesus;*[vi]

                  your pious words rile me;
                  self-serving, blind

how easily we split in two—

                what is kindness
                    without equality?

    Not slavery, but every day
    I nail down my superiority

over tip the $3 an hour server;
share cutie oranges with
the condo staff;

hand down computers
winter coats; once, a piano
to my undocumented trainer;

our two homes will go
to our children; I step over
the addict in the street.

Zebulon 1753	Nancy 2021
cock a	crow-struck I
doo	white woman
dle	can't muzzle
doo	your rooster sound
a-doo	
adoodle	your code
doo	your call
	I want
cocka doo	to climb up
	talk with you
a doo	you won't
cock a	let me speak
doodle	the sound you
doo	choose
cock	chokes me
a doo	
cocka	your voice
doodle	disallows
doo	my squawks
a doodle doo	I hear you

[My ancestor] Michael St. Agnan was drowned while bringing back to Trinidad a cargo of African slaves from the mainland of Latin America. This tragic event...[vii]

Michael, I refuse to let you curl
    silent on the ocean shelf, brass buttons
    turned green, beneath black bodies strewn
    among rusted chains and rum barrels.

I haul your ghost up from the brine
    stretch your shade out on the sand.
    Flies swarm, all these years waiting
    for you to surface.

Drowned 1821, you smuggler, you
    black marketeer.[viii] Let the sun parch
    your skeleton dry as the brown cursive
    of your human ledgers, promissory notes.

Cousin Jimmy elides this part, brags about
    your luster pitcher, tortoise-shell combs
    rimmed with gold, deep-toned mahogany
    on dusty display at Forty Acres.

No matter how I swat away the buzz
    tormenting me on kelp-striped sand,
    your ridged coins keep multiplying
    deep in my pockets.

July 12 1772 Wednesday a very Remarkable experience of Divine preservation. A flash of Lightenin came Down our Ketching Chimney almost filled the room with Flame. ...three persons in the room...our younest Negro Girl Phillis. All shocked but none hurt...the lightning melted trammel, hand iron, shovel and a spike left on the edge of the floor near the hearth[ix]

1989 Loma Prieta Quake: earth liquified, freeways crumbled, water from our swimming pool sloshed down the hill onto a neighbor's house. I called on the insurance company not the Divine.

The day Zebulon crowed
from the steeple, the Gazette
reported him as Elizabeth Phelps'
African man. Not Mende or
Igbo. Not son of Arthur Prutt
of nearby Amherst.

Which African ancestors of his
survived the 80 days, 18-inch
berth?

Archives digitized, I might
trace the very ship, bill of lading,
auction tag. Who am I
to dig through these drawers?
Expose a birthname, village
raider or telltale bead.

Do I want to know the first
price, first port, if mine
were shipbuilders, bookkeepers
clerks who kept the ledgers?

Dormant in each molasses keg
and bit of crockery, iron ballast,
broken mast or gold doubloon:
the waters brine us all.

Run away from the Widow Elizabeth Porter of Hadley, a Negro Man named Zebulon Prut, about 30 years old, about five Feet high, a whitish Complexion, suppos'd to have a Squaw in Company...

I never expected Zebulon to be "whitish." Or so small. How many of us white readers made him into some movie image? A Sydney or Denzel.

I remember how my former husband Mel struggled being light-skinned. Shoved aside by black and white.

Carried away with him, a light brown Camblet Coat, lin'd and trimm'd with the same Colour—a plain Cloth Coat, with Metal Buttons, without Lining—a new redish brown plain Cloth Coat, with Plate Buttons, no Lining—a light brown Waistcoat, and a dark brown ditto, both without Sleves—a Pair of Check'd and a Pair of Tow Trowsers—a Pair of blue Yarn Stockings, and a Pair of Thread ditto—two Pair of Shoes—two Hats—an old red Duffel Great Coat—whoever will take up said Negro, and bring him to Mrs. Porter, or to Oliver Warner, of said Hadley shall have Ten Dollars Reward, and all necessary Charges paid by Oliver Warner....

Elizabeth, you practically grew up with him. Say nothing in your Diary about his running away. Only his capture a year later, "slave owned by my father."

My saying nothing. When the garage attendant called Mel "boy." Saying nothing. When he was overlooked by his white boss. Saying nothing. When, after the divorce, our 16-year-old son's white therapist told him it was "okay to pass for white."

O how ought my heart to be humbled, low in the dust before God, that the privilege which I so ardently desired, & confidently expected, has been almost wholly denied me.

Elizabeth, decades of weekly
diary-keeping: Rev. Hopkins' sermons,
chores, visitors, deaths, births,
pounds of cheese you made. Rarely
do you burst out like this:

That you married expecting a helpmate
to build a church that welcomed
squire and maltster, gravedigger and slave
passing the two-handled communion cup.

That you *ardently desired* Charles
mull a Bible verse with you,
late into the night. Instead,
he strode in the reflection of
those silver communion cups he donated.

I married Mel, sure as any
cum laude white Smithie could be,
that the world would accept
ebony grannies, freckle-sprayed Dads,
tawny aunts, mothers fishbelly-pale,
babies honeyed as maple.

When I paraded our infant boy
to the Cobble Hill butcher, *Wow
you've got breasts,* exclaimed Joe
who taught me the difference

between brisket and loin. About our son,
not a word.

Mel and I argued Malcom versus
Martin, Panthers or busing. But did I
understand what it took for him—
a black man in the 60's art scene—
to put his images into that world?

Today I swivel my chair, look out
my tower windows, the view
bridge to bridge over San Francisco Bay.
In Jamaica I bumbled my way
with *higglers* in the market, Rasta
artists. Felt the friction of my skin
on the bus, at the bank.

Elizabeth, your diary proves
you never missed a Sunday service,
rode out at midnight to assist women
in labor, raised an orphan girl you named
Thankful.

My Calvinist streak chastises,
Why am I not doing more?

Like you, like my mother.
At 95, she was still
standing on the corner,
the weekly peace vigil.

Her Dixie cup candle—
one small flame
in the wind.

Dec 22, 1771 Last Tuesday cesar froze his finger June 4, 1775 ...Cesar has had a terrible Swelled hand this month...May it be for his spiritual good.[xi]

Cesar can't lift his hand;
nor the axe or tap the maples;

        Elizabeth: get your medicine box;
        the wooden one, reeking camphor
        and chamomile;

a "woman of your station"
tends to those in need;

     I was a hospital candy striper
     at age 12; Girl Scout badge;
     also training

   lift your skirts over the mud;
   enter any door;

        your husband sent swole-handed Cesar
        to fight in his place at Fort Ticonderoga;

you couldn't save enslaved baby Phillis
from King's Evil; nor her namesake;[xii]

     I volunteer as End of Life
     Counselor; ease the last hours;

can't help questioning
the power I feel,
a life in my hands

     did you feel it too, Elizabeth—
     the power of your station?

1659-1808. Well documented,
we enslaved 7 people: Sue,
Zebulon, Cesar, Peg, her children
who died: Rose, Phillis, grandbaby Phillis.
And then

summer 2021,
in the Phelps' Barn—
a grad student uncovered
stacks of receipts, bills of lading,
adventures*[*] tied in 6 neat bundles.
Untouched, unread since 1870.
Signed Charles Phelps,
Elizabeth's only son,

who failed at law in Boston, ventured
into the export trade. One receipt reads
> shipped in good order and condition
> Phelps and Rand in ship called Great America
> ... bound for Copenhagen 32 hogsheads
> of sugar weighing 15 tons 735 pounds.

Cane born of sweat, starvation, fingers sliced to shreds.
217,000 Africans in Cuba alone; few survived 7 years;
2 crops a year, round-the-clock, sugar mills cannot stop.

By 1812, 600 U.S. ships sailed from Havana
with the sticky sweet, threading between
Napoleon's dragoons, England's navy.

Every receipt stamped "citizen of United States"
to protect ships from seizure, sailors from capture.
Charles' profit: $12.7 million in today's dollars.

---

*a type of receipt listing the commodity, ship name, port, captain

Untie another packet; receipts reveal
Georgia cotton, on the *Rebecca.*
What of the bent backs, families rent,
forced breeding, bruises?

No comments in Charles' letters on the abolitionist
fervor bubbling in Boston. He worries about
his debts, cost of living, raising capital.

Records his 10 terms in the State Legislature,
3 wives who died, their 8 children. Says
he is "self-made."

Not a nod to the lives whittled into
sugar crystals, fingers that twisted
free each boll, 200,000 to a bail.
No mention of ships unloading
millions of Africans

to plantations far from the cool
green of Hadley. The steel-blue
Atlantic breaks my tidy shore.

From bare
shoulders, I
want him

to spring
iridescent
feathers,
green, red,
black. I
want him
to wing out
his arms,
swoop

III. The Rupture

My Puritan White Skin

Inspired by "Big Gay Ass Poem", B.C. Griffiths

City Walgreens, plate glass, sunshine. Single clerk, single line.
    Customer's wig: white peaks of frosting against blue-black skin,
    clerk's brown cheek and close-cropped Afro.

They chat—smile, unload—
    cart piled high.

I'm waiting to ask the checker, *Where are the razor blades?*
I must be blind

Did I sigh? Shift my weight?

The customer glares my way   cocks her head
    The   line   forms
    behind me

I jump into place a good ten feet back   cheeks surge red
    Stand there   feels like an hour
can't bear it
    bolt from the store

Pound down the street. Never get it right, thought I was polite
    off to the side, measured my distance.

Stop dead, mid-stride.
It wasn't just *me* in that line, sun pouring in. It was my skin,
my Puritan white skin.

No wonder I jumped out of mine—
turned inside out, back of the line.

Skin, I must remember to see you
though I've lived long in your pale veneer. Trail of DNA,

America since 1639. Cousin here, cousin there,
look-alikes everywhere. That shiver
when other skin colors show up.

Remember Harlem, '64 after the riots,
men jeered Whitey at you clutching
your welfare-worker casebook on Lennox Avenue.

Three years in Kingston, Jamaica, the epithet *Pawk*
after the white meat of the pig.
Bus ride, straphanging teens snicker. Smell of their armpits,
over you.

Sure you've grown callous
but I'm appealing to your soft side.
Tender when I smooth sunscreen
on you every morning. I love you
all age-spotted, all you've been through.

No blame for carrying this DNA.
But let's tell the truth.
Not ashamed or blind.

We *did* plant our skinflag at the head of the line.
Used to that spot. Used to getting what we want
and being loved at the same time.

Did the customer peel out of the store,
exhausted by skin, too?
Was she furious, exhilarated? I can't know.

White skin, sit still with me
on this bench. Feel the rupture—
white and black. How deep
the wound. Its raggedy lips.
Let's start here.

Sweet Boy From Chicago

Emmett Till   1941-1955

Not this bitter metal
Nor men white-peaked
No men in sheets looming
No cave eyes behind torn holes
No white wimmin
No looking   ever   no N.... never
No rules in the night   neither
Screams nor barbed wire ratchet
No hoods in his great uncle's face
Nor sweat-tight back   knee buckles
No cicadas screaming

Nor me, this white girl fourteen like him   eyes meeting eyes
In the newspaper
Not Mississippi   nor Chicago
But New England   not black like him
No looking
No sweet smile   fedora Chicago style
Nor his fingers   where are his fingers?
Nor his eyes gouged out
Chicago snow   where is his snow?

Not Mississippi's smother   honeysuckle cloy
No rules rubbing off
Neither his face no face
Chicago boy
Fourteen, like me
Not me

Fraying Bridge

Rope twisted and hairy   on this fraying bridge
   don't trust   even a first step—

12 years, no word, no reason   a canyon between you
   and   our only child

   Today—your email to him:

   —even if a gale rocks the bridge
if you dangle mid-air—grab

                his hand, the rough rail

     — this most fragile
of conversations.   You say not

   father to son   only as equals.

      (How can he not be your son?)

Brown and Tager's 360 pp.
Concise History of Massachusetts,
published in 2000 by the University
of Massachusetts Press, makes no
mention of slave-holding and slave trading
in colonial Massachusetts.[xiv]

shining
and crowing
in my head

Pries
my
voice
from
white
pages

Coming Upon This Tree in the Open Space

Stark grey limbs scrape the blue off the sky,
roots wedge under boulders. Half-dead, hollow,
bark raked thin. Small brown birds twitter and hop.
                              I turn away

seek a leafy oak, a burst of poppies, anything
but the ugliness, the dull dread this tree
stirs up. My urge to stride past so strong
                              I make myself look—

the potency of avoidance. This summer of George Floyd,
this summer I discover my ancestors were enslavers.
Every twig, every burl on this tree reveals itself:
                              a strip-tease of racism.

Listen to the faint thuds of its possum heart,
bow my forehead against the ridged trunk.
Fragrant, the slow decay.
                              If it were only wood,

not my decomposing hope, its smell of
wet dog, the last burnt leaf of fall. Carried by
rough gusts
                              dead-still at midnight.

Lightning only charred the tree.
Its husk taunts
                              sly victory.

Fantasia on White Supremacy

I

One Sunday in church
Pony sidles up to me, tooths
the blue cotton of my sleeve and
tugs me out of Our Father.

No animals at the altar rail!
Don't you see the signs?

Pony shrugs his coppery coat,
ridding flies. I rise and follow
past bowed heads, rote mumblers.
Mute rooster spins bright atop the steeple,
flicks omens on the roof.

Pony noses me to the ground, trots
a circle tight around me. Roots
grow from my calves, lash me
to the churchyard.

White in the grass, clover
blooms out of reach.
He never takes his eyes off me.
Hub of his wheel.

Why bind me here, Pony
amid cow paths and Commons?

He nickers, lifts
his creamy tail, plops
golden balls of yarn.

Words upon words drone from
the chapel. The pony's saliva
dries on his toothmarks
jagged on my blue sleeve.

II

Pony, don't expect me to be perfect.
You pulled me from the pews,
what good if I can't move?

Fixed like a maypole, I am
eyes and mouth blinded by ribbons.
You have the legs, the haunches.

Drag me over stubble to the river.
Let the currents float us
through cattails and eelgrass.

I'll go last in crack-
the-whip; you can swing me
off the ground.

Let me straddle your spiny back
head against your mane.
We'll run and run.

This endless circuit, Pony
empties my mind like a
chamber pot.

III

Your rump grows dusty, the sheen goes off. Cockleburs
thatch your sweeping tail. Still, your sharp eyes pin me.

Those balls of shit baking in the sun. I
churn in boredom,

lose track, centuries or yesterday.
Your circling taunts.

Am I the one who refuses to unhitch
myself? let go my place in the center, fear

a wildness of hoots in the night, dances I don't know, words that leap
my bounds. Whose rules? Whose gods?

Pony darling, sweet-eared friend, I need you at my side.
Who else can love me after what I've done?

Three more circles, then let's go. No path, no map,
first footfalls into the half-light.

Thirteen Potencies

I
Word by word my ancestors build the white church
Copper rooster glints atop the steeple
Zebulon, our African man, clings to the spire and crows
Wind whips
All day on the Lower East Side stoop, I wait for Mel

II
Zebulon runs away with a Pequot lover
Mel paints the African diaspora and sees himself
Cyclones blow my blond hair
Years, I knit in a Windsor chair
Ripping up white clover, Pony trots the cow paths

III
Grandchildren seek out their estranged grandfather
The rooster greens with age
Hallelujah, Zebulon praises from his perch
I sweep the church with a corn-broom
Wind unravels the yarns

IV
Zebulon survives the pox house
Despite tan skin and curls, grandchildren join the D.A.R.
Steeple climbing is an Olympic sport
Mel could have been Zebulon
Pony elected Sheriff of Hampshire County

V
Back and forth, wind slaps the rooster
Mel makes tissue paper kites for his grandchildren
Cracks in the steeple, I raise money to repair it
Bumping and bellowing, the cows ruckus across the Commons
Zebulon free in Vermont

VI

My kin trace their DNA to Zeb and his Pequot partner
I strengthen my inner thighs, shimmy trees
The rooster shears off in Hurricane Sylvie
Mel's great-grandmother eludes a rapist overseer
Everywhere, white clover multiplies

VII

Mel does not run from his family
Zebulon climbs down to have tea with me
The grandchildren beg for family stories
In front of the church, a merry-go-round. Pony gallops away
Rooster refuses to abandon the wind

VIII

With his creamy tail Pony whisks flies off Widow Porter
Read Moses Porter's will: he frees Zebulon
The clover's overrun by witchgrass
Bony as rails, the congregation goes hungry
Mel's mother studies law in Montreal

IX

Zebulon hums "We Shall Overcome" in his rocking chair
Mel to son Adam, *Winter on the beach with me in Cabo*
I climb the steeple and crow
My grandchildren darken in the sun
Pony leaps the gables, grabs my collar, pulls me off the steeple

X

Pawk, Kingston teens taunt me, white in Jamaica
Paint peels off the church
Roxbury, I'm date-raped by a Black Nationalist
Zebulon lives to age 71
Rooster soars over the Great River

XI

Zebulon and Mel's skin: called red-bone, yellow-bone
Rooster shimmers copper in the sun
In a flaxen rage, Pony kicks down the church
The grandchildren are not Black
I root in white clover

XII

Mel rips my cover off when he leaves
Naked white girl, on her own
Zebulon sweats into the fibers of my ancestor's duffel. I remember.
Pony sheds coppery hairs, sparkles the clover
The wind becalms the Atlantic

XIII

Lips sealed, Pony circles
Zebulon crows unanswerable
Mel disappeared eighteen years ago
Our white-passing son mute on subject of race
I spin and spin, crow into this silence

Appendix

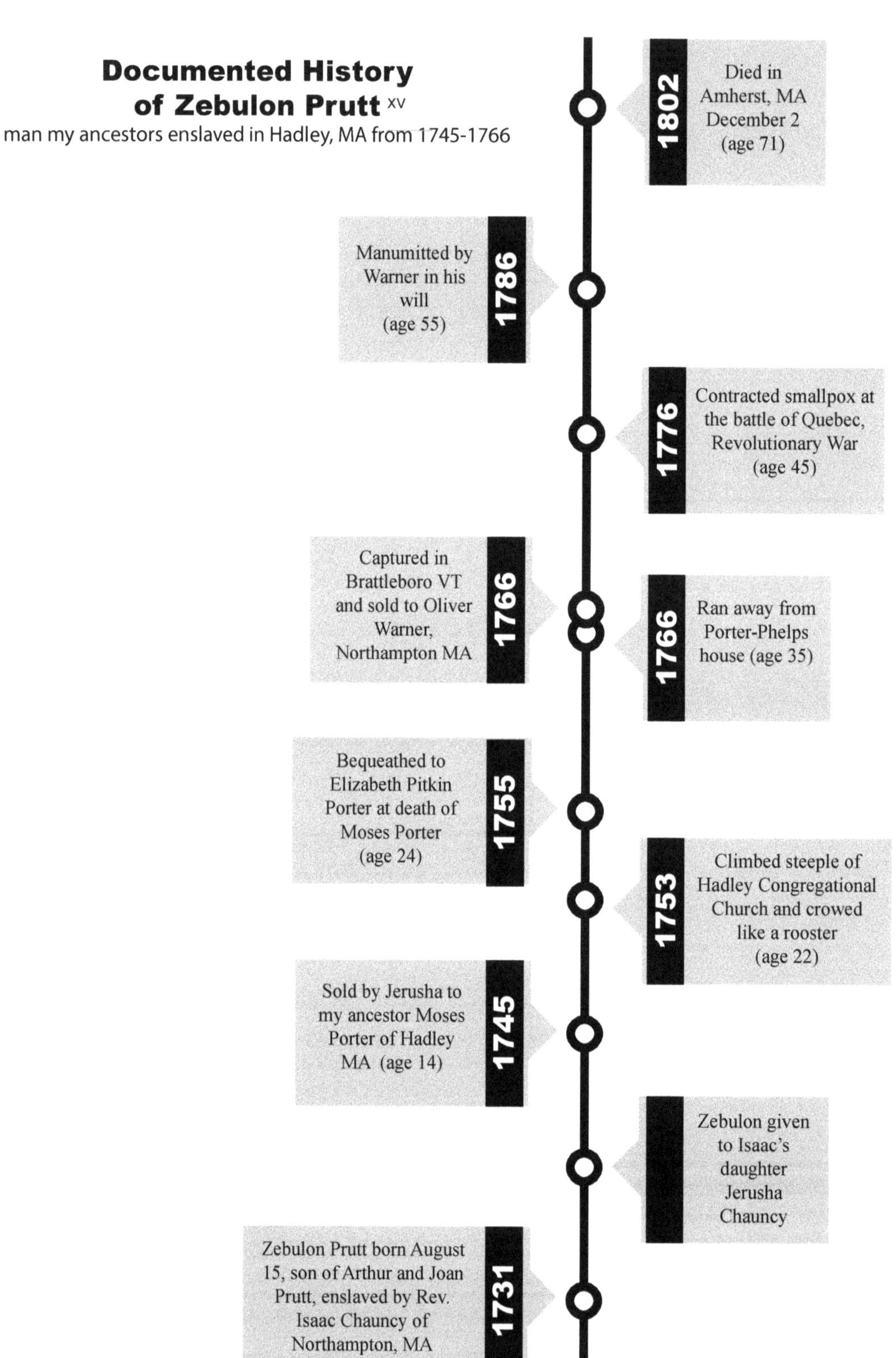

Documented History
of Zebulon Prutt xv
man my ancestors enslaved in Hadley, MA from 1745-1766
1802
Died in Amherst, MA December 2 (age 71)
1786
Manumitted by Warner in his will (age 55)
1776
Contracted smallpox at the battle of Quebec, Revolutionary War (age 45)
1766
Captured in Brattleboro VT and sold to Oliver Warner, Northampton MA
1766
Ran away from Porter-Phelps house (age 35)
1755
Bequeathed to Elizabeth Pitkin Porter at death of Moses Porter (age 24)
1753
Climbed steeple of Hadley Congregational Church and crowed like a rooster (age 22)
1745
Sold by Jerusha to my ancestor Moses Porter of Hadley MA (age 14)
Zebulon given to Isaac's daughter Jerusha Chauncy
1731
Zebulon Prutt born August 15, son of Arthur and Joan Prutt, enslaved by Rev. Isaac Chauncy of Northampton, MA

Works Cited

Carlisle, Elizabeth. *Earthbound and Heavenbent,* (New York, Scribner, 2004).

Huntington, James L. *Forty Acres, The Story of the Bishop Huntington House*, (New York, Hastings House, 1949).

Judd, Sylvester. *History of Hadley: Including the Early History of Hatfield, South Hadley, Amherst and Granby, Massachusetts* (Northampton: Metcalf & Co., 1863). My citations rely on a later edition published in Springfield, Mass., H. R. Huntting & company, 1905.

Phelps, Elizabeth Porter. *The Diary of Elizabeth (Porter) Phelps,* edited by Thomas Eliot Andrews with an introduction by James Lincoln Huntington in The New England Historical Genealogical Register. Boston: New England Historic Genealogical Society, Jan. 1964.

Porter, Phelps, Huntington Museum website, www.pphmuseum.org

Romer, Robert. *Slavery in the Connecticut Valley of Massachusetts,* (Northampton, Levelers Press, 2009)

Author's Note

I found my initial information from a family copy of James L. Huntington's book *Forty Acres, The Story of the Bishop Huntington House,* where my grandmother took me as a child. The website of the Porter-Phelps-Huntington Foundation (www.pphmuseum. org) adds valuable scholarship and benefits from the archiving of 200 years of our family papers at Special Collections & University Archives at the University of Massachusetts (SCUA). The website contains a generous bibliography that expands on both our family history, that of the surrounding Connecticut River Valley and the contributions of enslaved and indigenous peoples. The Diary of my 8th-great-grandmother Elizabeth Porter Phelps is housed at SCUA.

[i] Robert Romer, *Slavery in the Connecticut Valley of Massachusetts,* Levelers Press, 2009. Appendix 1, p. 237

[ii] https://www.pphmuseum.org/in-elizabeths-words-blog/2019/6/29/october-11-1772

[iii] Elizabeth Porter Phelps Diary, https://www.pphmuseum.org/work-and-community

[iv] https://elizabeth-porter-8edg.squarespace.com/letters-of-the-porters

[v] Elizabeth Carlisle, *Earthbound and Heavenbent*, p. 315. Seventh sons were believed to have second sight, as well as the power to cure diseases in addition to scrofula, beliefs that were carried with the early settlers from Britain.

[vi] Elizabeth Carlisle, *Earthbound and Heavenbent,* p. 104.

[vii] James L. Huntington, *Forty Acres,* p 37

[viii] International slave trade banned in 1808

[ix] Elizabeth Carlisle, *Earthbound and Heavenbent,* pp 63, 64

[x] https://www.pphmuseum.org/slavery-and-servitude-at-forty-acres-blog/2018/8/26/finally-freedom-peg-and-zebulon-at-forty-acres

[xi] Elizabeth Carlisle, *Earthbound and Heavenbent,* p. 65

[xii] https://www.pphmuseum.org/slavery-and-servitude-at-forty-acres-blog/2018/7/23/phillis-rose-and-phillis-slaves-and-illness-at-forty-acres

[xiii] "Come with Receipts:" Charles Porter Phelps and the Atlantic Sugar Trade recorded by Alison Russsell at Porter, Phelps, Huntington Museum on July 25, 2022

[xiv] Robert Romer, *Slavery in the Connecticut Valley of Massachusetts,* p. 237

[xv] Graphics by Stephanie Pressman; text by Nancy L Meyer 2022 from source material on www.pphmuseum.org and Sylvester Judd, *History of Hadley*

Questions for Reflection or Group Discussion

A Note From Nancy

I would love this work to open up reflection about your own experiences across race and cultures. During the eight years of this project, I have uncovered more of my white biases and ignorance of history. I hope to trigger your curiosity, even action.

Here are some questions that ran through my mind while I wrote the book. I have paired them with selected poems to provide focus.

In a group you might choose poems and topics to explore. For each topic, read aloud the poems. Enter the conversation with one or two others for a given time and then return to the whole group to share highlights and expand the discussion.

Cross-Race Relations and Identity

1. How do you connect or separate from others in cross-racial, cross-cultural relationships. **"Wedding Album," "Out of Many, One People," "Fraying Bridge"**

2. What do you think has changed, or not changed, in the United States regarding cross-racial relationships since the1963-1983 period of my first marriage? **"Alone, Sweet Boy from Chicago," "The Stoop," "About That Jamaican Wedding Cake"**

3. How did the integration movement serve U.S. society? Where did it fall short? **"Wedding Album," "Between Our Lips," "LL Bean Boots, Navy Surplus Pants, Hair to My Waist"**

4. Explore the pitfalls and benefits of our focus on identity especially in mixed-race relationships. **"Recant," "Out of Many, One People," "Grieve but Cannot Grieve"**

5. In what ways do you seek like-minded, like-looking others in your life? Where do you engage with those less like yourself? What is the impact of your choices? **"Higglers," "Dreaming Jamaica," "Two Marriages"**

Family Legacy

1. How does your family describe itself? What happens when new information upends that story? **"Story Keeper," "Zebulon on the Steeple"**

2. What family stories do you NOT tell? **"Text Fragment: Ad in Connecticut Courant, Sep. 8, 1766"**

3. What are your reactions to intergenerational wealth? if you have some where did it come from? if not, why not. **"Text Fragment: Accounting", "Read the Receipts"**

4. What patterns of behavior or life choices do you see passed down in your family? How many generations back can you trace these? **"Diary Fragment: Seventh Son", "Diary Fragment: Medicine Box," "Diary Fragment 37th Wedding Anniversary, June 14, 1807"**

5. What do you think our 8th-great-grandchildren would say about us today?

Can We Change?

1. Imagine experiencing a change in your social position, what fears or expectations arise? **"My Puritan White Skin," "Fear Rider Series"**

2. People often respond to me as if my comments indicate guilt or shame for my behavior or that of my ancestors. Can guilt or shame motivate as well as shut us down? **"Fear Rider Series," "Coming Upon This Tree in the Open Space"**

3. How do you manage your discomfort or fear in unfamiliar encounters? *"Steeple Monologue,"* **"Higglers"**

4. How do you open your eyes to perspectives you may have missed, so you can move in the world with more integrity? **"My Puritan White Skin," "It Wasn't Only Race That Ended Us," "Erased"**

Acknowledgments

I am grateful for the editors of the following publications where a version of these poems first appeared:

BeZine: "My Puritan White Skin," "Recant," "Response to Elizabeth Porter Phelps Diary Fragment: Seventh Son"

Black Moon Magazine: "The Wedding Album: 1965"

Book of Matches: "Between Our Lips," "Patoos Croon in the Frangipani Tree"

Caesura: My 8th-Great-Grandmother Elizabeth Porter Phelps Diary Fragment: 37th Wedding Anniversary June 14, 1807

Common Ground: "Fraying Bridge," "Coming Upon This Tree in Open Space"

Crossing Class Anthology, Wising Up Press: "Higglers"

DeColonial Passage: "Read the Receipts"

Feral A Journal of Poetry and Art: "Fall"

International Human Rights Arts Festival: "All Our Stories Come Ashore," "Text Fragment: Ad in Connecticut Courant, Sep. 8, 1766"

Last Stanza Poetry Journal: "Dreaming Jamaica," "Grieve But Cannot Grieve"

Laurel Review: "After the Laurentide"

Madison Review: "This Endless Circuit, Pony" now part of "Fear Rider "

McNeese Review: "Native Waters"

Muleskinner Journal: "Our Family's First Century in Hadley," "Story Keeper," "Response to Text Fragment: Accounting"

Museum of Americana: A Literary Review: "LL Bean Boots, Navy Surplus Pants, Hair to My Waist."

Nebraska Poetry Society Open Contest: Third Place winner, "About That Jamaican Wedding Cake."

New Note Poetry: "Steeple Monologues"

Outcast Press: "Our Love Blew Apart Like a Pinata"

The Other Journal: "Text Fragment: Zebulon on the Steeple"

Wordland:Black Is The New Black: "Sweet Boy From Chicago"

Write Launch: "Alone," "The Night After I Stumbled upon My Blood Owning Slaves"

Gratitude

All love to my good husband Chris, for his kind witness as I rummaged through my first marriage to write this book. And to our sons and their children, my greatest blessings and hope for the world.

Deep gratitude goes to Rusty Morrison of Omnidawn Press who has mentored me throughout this project and to Maw Shein Win who added invaluable perspective in my final lap. A bow to Jeffrey Levine, of Tupelo Press and to Sally Ashton. Emeritus Professor of San Jose State, constant and pivotal teachers who helped me call myself, poet. The skill and attention of Stephanie Pressman editor of Frog on the Moon made the glide-path to publication a joy.

A first reader is invaluable. Kudos to Kate Utt who receives rough drafts with keen psychological insight only an old friend and sister poet can offer.

I am indebted to my grandmother's cousin, Dr. James Huntington, for founding The Porter-Phelps-Huntington Museum and to the Special Collections and University Archives at U.Mass which house our family documents and laid a rich table for my poetic appetite. A shout-out to the many researchers who have written vividly about the men and women who settled, owned or labored on this property.

This project required a deep dive into my unconscious racism. I was prompted to keep digging by the workshop, *Healing Racism Within* led by Cynthia Zeltwanger, Ann Litwin and Rima Imburgia, the models in Rianna Moore's *Journeys of Race, Color, & Culture* and the wise training of Ruth King. Since 1993 I have committed with the Women's Community Leadership Collaborative to embrace our differences with open eyes and heart. This work has changed my life.

I could not have completed this journey without the genius of my several poetry groups. Thank you: Kara Arguello, Jade Bradbury, Jessica Cohn, Mary Anne Cook, Irene Cooper, Kelly Cressio-Moeller, Rocky de laPlaine, Lora Kincade, Hilary King, Veronica Kornberg, Linda Lancione, Catherine Latta, Jean Lin, Kathie Isaac-Luke, Nancy Mohr, Philip Periman, Stephanie Pressman, William Rudolph, Mary Ann Savage, Ariel Smart, Cathy Wright. And to the memories of Jean Emerson, Elaine Kahn, Judy Oppenheimer, Mary Lou Taylor, Bernis Terhune and Phyllis Williams.

About the Author

Nancy L Meyer, she/her, settled in the unceded Ramaytush Ohlone lands of the San Francisco Bay Area in 1977. Raised in 1950's Massachusetts in a family of mixed religion, class, and a far-left political philosophy, she was often "the other" in school or social groups. She came of age during the Civil Rights era, marched in Selma, married a Jamaican and raised their son in the U.S. and Jamaica. Well into her second marriage, Nancy found family documents exposing a colonial legacy of slave-holding and enrichment from the slave economy. She wrote *The Stoop and The Steeple* in response to this discovery and its upending of her family mythology as progessives, descended from educators, artists and farmers.

Writing helps me expose disparate fragments and make new wholes, Nancy says, describing herself as a late-life poet. She began to write after retiring as a social worker, women's leadership educator and organization development consultant in healthcare.

She has published poems in over 50 journals in the United States and United Kingdom, including T*upelo Quarterly, The Colorado, McNeese, Laurel and Sugar House Reviews, Feral,* and *Halfway Down the Stairs.* She is also included in nine anthologies and is a recipient of a Hedgebrook Residency.

Follow Nancy at
nancylmeyerpoet at Facebook and Instagram, and
www.NancyLMeyer.com.

For your notes: